West Country Engine Sheds

Maurice Dart

Ian Allan 60th ANNIVERSARY

First published 2002

ISBN 0 7110 2904 0

Published by Ian Allan Publishing

an imprint of Ian Allan Publishing Ltd, Hersham, Surrey KT12 4RG
Printed by Ian Allan Printing Ltd, Hersham, Surrey KT12 4RG

Code: 0209/B1

Acknowledgements

I would like to thank the various photographers and collectors who have granted me permission to use their work or items from their collections in this book, with special thanks to Mike Daly and Mr R. C. Riley for their help with the colour material. My thanks are also extended to the numerous railwaymen who, in the past, allowed me to visit sheds and to take photographs. I would also like to thank Sally Webb for help in the initial stages of using my word processor and also I am deeply grateful to Malcolm Surl of Luxsoft for his work on my disk. Lastly, my thanks go to Eric Youldon for assistance on certain points and also to Brian Rose of Ian Allan Publishing for his encouragement with this project.

Front cover: 'M7' class 0-4-4T No 30667 stands over a pit outside Exmouth Junction shed in glorious afternoon sun on 7 April 1963. This locomotive is not quite what it appears as the original No 30667 was withdrawn in November 1960, and in March 1961 No 30106 returned to traffic, ex works renumbered as 30667. *Maurice Dart*

Back cover: The sub-shed at Moorswater on 17 March 1960. Prairie No 4552 is seen passing the shed which served the Looe branch. *R. C. Riley*

Title page:
An overview of Penzance shed, showing the main building, the 'Factory', and pump house. Locomotives in the yard include 'Castle', 'Hall', 'Grange', 'Manor' and 'County' class 4-6-0s and a '4500' class 2-6-2T along with the breakdown train, which is stabled to the left of the shed building in this 9 April 1960 view. *R. C. Riley*

Contents

Reference Sources

The Handbook of Steam Motive Power Depots, Volume 1: Southern England, Paul Smith. Platform 5 Publishing

An Historical Survey of Great Western Engine Sheds 1947, E. Lyons, Oxford Publishing Co

GWR Locomotive Allocations. First and Last Sheds, 1922-1967, J. W. P. Rowledge. David & Charles

British Railways Locomotive Stock Changes and Withdrawal Dates, 1948-1968, Volumes One, Two, Three and Five. Michael MacManus

The Xpress Locomotive Register, Volumes One, Two and Four, Xpress Publishing

London & South Western Railway Engine Sheds, Western District, Chris Hawkins & George Reeve. Irwell Press

Locomotives of the GWR, various parts, Railway Correspondence & Travel Society

BR Steam Motive Power Depots: SR, Paul Bolger, Ian Allan

Branch Line to Padstow and *Branch Lines to Falmouth, Helston and St Ives*, both by Vic Mitchell & Keith Smith, Middleton Press

My own notebooks dating from 1945.

Introduction

My first knowledge of engine sheds was gained at a tender age, when, on my 'O' gauge model railway, I had an 'engine house' which my father had made. Subsequently, during trips to Plymouth from our home at St Budeaux, locomotives were always to be seen before we reached the station, at what I later learned was Millbay shed. Each August in 1937, 1938 and 1939, we had a South Devon Runabout ticket and usually headed for Paignton, Torquay, Kingswear or Dawlish Warren during the week. It was on these journeys that I had my first sightings of Laira shed as we passed, and I was told: 'That is where the engines live'. I asked if we could go there some time, but my wish was not granted at that time; probably because I was only seven years of age. More locomotives were of course seen at Newton Abbot, including the 'bulletnose' No 5005 *Manorbier Castle*.

During the war, I was first evacuated to Bude, where I was able to gaze from the front bedroom window across the marshes to see several locomotives, including 'N' class 2-6-0s gathered around the small locomotive shed.

Following a short spell back at St Budeaux, I was evacuated to St Austell where I met more railway enthusiasts from Plymouth and my 'railway education' commenced properly. This culminated in a trip one Sunday afternoon to Par from where we found our way to the path, actually on the trackbed of the Treffry Tramway, which we followed until we were opposite the locomotive shed at St Blazey. From this vantage point we were able to identify all the locomotives in the yard, on the coaling line and also those inside the front of the shed as their numbers were displayed in gold figures on both the front and rear buffer beams.

At the end of the war, I returned to St Budeaux and was very soon introduced by pals to Laira shed. A public footpath ran along the side of the roundhouse and past the coaling line to a bridge beneath the main and relief lines, which gave a good view of part of the shed complex. One could go beyond the bridge a short way to reach the shed yard throat where sleepers, which formed part of the side of the trackbed, made very convenient seats for us. I used to peer through the windows of the roundhouse to try to identify the locomotives inside, usually ending with a black tip to my nose. After a few visits, I was shown how to enter the shed by squeezing through some railings and going around the rear of the buildings, past the one-road 'Factory', to reach the back of the 'New' or 'Long' shed, which was open-ended.

A doorway then led into the roundhouse where we went around the outside of the locomotives, retracing our steps into the New shed from where we walked out through the extensive yard and crossed the lines at the shed throat to take up our usual perch. Such was my introduction to the delights of visiting locomotive sheds. The foremen at Laira were quite friendly, but, as I was to discover, this was not the case at all sheds.

Devon and Cornwall were well provided with locomotive sheds, although some held only one or two locomotives, but every shed had its own characteristics. Locomotive sheds were fascinating places to visit, not only to

Right:
'West Country' class 4-6-2 No 34011 *Tavistock*, from Plymouth Friary shed, has worked up to Exeter Central on a portion of the 'Devon Belle' and has come on shed at Exmouth Junction for coaling and turning on 8 July 1949. The water treatment tank is high above the shed roof, and a line of old tenders used for sludge removal is in the right background.
Maurice Dart collection

record the engines present but also to see their preparation and servicing being carried out, together with the facilities and equipment for doing so. Inside the sheds some locomotives could he found carrying notices stating 'NOT TO BE MOVED', and, inevitably, various sections of their pistons or other rodding would be on the shed floor or on a workbench nearby. Other locomotives would have hoses connected to various places and carry a chalked legend stating 'WASH OUT', while others might have their smokebox door open with some boiler tubes removed. Maintaining steam locomotives in those conditions was arduous, awkward, heavy and dirty work, usually performed under rather poor lighting; trailing leads with a bulb affixed could be seen on locomotives under repair. The floor of the shed was usually covered by a variety of hoses, rods, shovels, heavy hammers, metal wheelbarrows and trolleys.

Great care was required when going around any shed. At Laira, I once saw a young enthusiast attempt to jump across an inspection pit with raised rails, to save walking around it, resulting in him crashing partly into it and breaking a vein in his leg, which of course created problems for the shed staff. Another factor which added to the sensation experienced when visiting a shed was the ever-present smell of a combination of hot lubricating oil, grease and smoke.

Other thoughts which preceded a shed visit were the anticipation of finding a local engine which had eluded me for some time, a type of locomotive new to the particular shed, or better still, the sight of a locomotive from a faraway shed which had either worked in after being 'borrowed' by another shed or had been sent 'on loan' for a period to cover a local shortage. This could be due to the shed's own locomotives being under repair or at times when a shed's turntable was undergoing some work and the normal tender locomotives could not be turned.

I will now look at each of the various sheds in the area and recall my experiences during visits to them, followed by a list of the locomotives seen on two visits. This may well produce examples such as those mentioned above. Locomotives listed without depot allocations in brackets were at their home shed.

Above:
At the back end of a line of withdrawn locomotives at Exmouth Junction shed is '8750' class 0-6-0PT No 3679 keeping company with 'M7' class 0-4-4T No 30125 on 7 April 1963. *Maurice Dart*

Above:
In the yard at Exmouth Junction shed, awaiting transfer to Yeovil Town, is ex-GWR '6400' class 0-6-0PT No 6412 on 22 December 1963. *Maurice Dart*

72A Exmouth Junction — EXJ/72A/83D from 9/9/63

I first visited this large shed during 1950. On my early visits I either went by bus or walked from Exeter Central station, and then passed through a gate in the fence on the right side of the approach road and walked down through the Southern's concrete works to the shed and yard. It was a 14-road long shed with a one-road lifting shop on the west side, adjoining the shed office. The yard was quite extensive with coaling and servicing facilities on the east side, next to the main lines. Later, the method of entry was to go to the end of the approach road and into the rear of the shed, commencing on the side furthest from the office. However, as the years progressed, we simply went to the office and saw the foreman and were never refused access, although on one occasion in the mid-1950s I met the foreman as I was just finishing going around and was told that I should not be in there, and was asked to leave.

On a Sunday, the yard usually contained many lines of locomotives, most of which were Bulleid Pacifics and 'N' class Moguls, while most of the small tank locomotives were to be found on the east side of the shed. There were also a couple of locomotives usually inside the lifting shop.

I recall on one visit I had almost completed going around the shed and had stopped to watch some work being carried out on a 'King Arthur' class 4-6-0. The fitter who was doing the work turned around and looked at me and told me that I had better shave before I went there again, otherwise he thought I may get caught up in the locomotive's wheels and rods. I should add that I was at

Above:
A Sunday afternoon c1958 finds the yard at Exmouth Junction shed filled with locomotives, including 'T9' class 4-4-0 No 30717 and 'N' class 2-6-0 No 31834 at the end of two of the shed roads. The roof of the lifting shop is high above the main shed building. *Mike Daly*

Above:
'N' class 2-6-0 No 31834 stands beside 'T9' class 4-4-0 No 30717 in front of Exmouth Junction shed, c1958. *Mike Daly*

that strange age when I was attempting to defer the onset of shaving regularly, but suffice to say I heeded his words.

I had an interesting visit to the shed when the entire class of 'Merchant Navy' Pacifics was withdrawn for examination of their axles in 1953, which produced some unusual sightings.

With such a large allocation, changes occurred continuously, even among the ex-SR types, some of which were gradually replaced by Ivatt 2-6-2Ts, followed by BR Standard 2-6-2Ts and 2-6-4Ts, so a visit to this shed usually produced something different.

The locomotives used for snowplough duties varied, with 'N' class 2-6-0s being followed in turn by '0395', '700' and 'Q' class 0-6-0s and ex-GWR '2251' class 0-6-0s.

Likewise, the locomotives used for banking duties between St Davids and Exeter Central stations changed, with 'E1/R' class 0-6-2Ts replaced by, in turn, 'Z' class 0-8-0Ts, 'W' class 2-6-4Ts and ex-GWR '8750' class 0-6-0PTs, the latter a development of the well-known '5700' class.

The shed was always referred to locally as 'The Junction', and I seem to have visited it no fewer than 24 times.

Above:
In the yard at Exmouth Junction shed in this 1950s photograph are 'M7' class 0-4-4T No 30323 and 'T9' class 4-4-0s Nos 30711 and 30712. *Maurice Dart collection*

Sunday, 24 May 1953

Class 0395 0-6-0	30564/75/80
Class 0415 4-4-2T	30582/83
Class E1/R 0-6-2T	32124/35, 32695/97
Class M7 0-4-4T	30021/25/41/42/45, 30323/56/57/74/75, 30669/76.
Class N15 4-6-0	30450 (72B)
Class O2 0-4-4T	30199
Class S15 4-6-0	30505/07 (both 70B), 30841/44/45
Class N 2-6-0	31831/32/33/36/41/45/47/48/49
Class T9 4-4-0	30709/10
Class U 2-6-0	31790 (72C)
Class U1 2-6-0	31896 (75B)
Class Z 0-8-0T	30954
Class WC/BB 4-6-2	34018/20 (both 70A), 34021/22/23/25/31, 34040 (71G), 34052/54 (both 72B), 34057/58/59, 34064/65 (both 70A), 34092 (73A)
Class MN 4-6-2	35001/02/04
Class 2 2-6-2T	41313/17
Class V2 2-6-2	60896 (36A), 60916 (35A), 60928 (36A)
Class 7P/6F 4-6-2	70024 (83D), 70028/29 (both 86C)
Class 3 2-6-2T	82014/17
Diesel Co-Co	10000 (70A)

Sunday, 7 April 1963

Class 700 0-6-0	30689/97, 30700 (all Wdn)
Class M7 0-4-4T	30025, 30125 (Wdn), 30667
Class N 2-6-0	31406/09, 31818/38/40/41/42/43/46/47/48/55/60/75
Class Q 0-6-0	30530/31
Class Z 0-8-0T	30951
Class S15 4-6-0	30841/45
Class W 2-6-4T	31911/12/14/15/16/24
Class MN 4-6-2	35010/22/26, 35018/24 (both 70A)
Class WC/BB 4-6-2	34015/30/34/36/58/62/69/75/79/81/83/86, 34091 (70E), 34106/09
Class 8750 0-6-0PT	3679, 3794 (83C), 4655/94
Class 2 2-6-2T	41238/70/89, 41306/07/08/18/21/23
Class 4 2-6-4T	80035/36/37/40/41/43/59/64
Type 2 diesel B-B	D6320 (83D)

Shed Codes

35A New England, Peterborough; 36A Doncaster; 70A Nine Elms; 70B Feltham; 70E and 72B both Salisbury; 71G Weymouth; 72C Yeovil Town; 73A Stewarts Lane; 75B Redhill; 83C Exeter; 83D Laira; 86C Cardiff Canton; Wdn Withdrawn

Above:
With the lifting shop at Exmouth Junction shed towering above it, Rebuilt 'Merchant Navy' class 4-6-2 No 35009 *Shaw Savill* stands alongside '0415' class Adams 'Radial' 4-4-2T No 30582 in front of the shed on 28 August 1957. *Maurice Dart collection*

Above right:
The new order has arrived at Exmouth Junction shed where a North British Type 2 diesel-hydraulic stands beside 'S15' class 4-6-0 No 30824 from Salisbury shed, c1963. *Maurice Dart collection*

Above:
A general view of the shed at Exmouth Junction on 20 September 1960, with the lifting shop on the left and the water treatment plant towering above the shed roof. Locomotives visible are, from left to right, 'M7' class 0-4-4T No 30670, 'S15' class 4-6-0 No 30845, 'West Country' class 4-6-2 No 34108 *Wincanton*, BR Standard Class 3 2-6-2T No 82019, 'West Country' class No 34096 *Trevone* and 'Merchant Navy' class 4-6-2 No 35013 *Blue Funnel*. *Maurice Dart collection*

Above left:
Standing on the ash road at Exmouth Junction shed on 22 December 1963 is 'S15' class 4-6-0 No 30825 of Salisbury shed. Behind the locomotive's tender is one of the shed's cranes, which was fitted with a bucket to scoop up ash. *Maurice Dart*

Above right:
On 6 December 1964 Ivatt Class 2 2-6-2T No 41216 stands beside the shed building at Exmouth Junction, next to the breakdown train. The water-softening tank stands high above the shed. *Maurice Dart*

Left:
BR Standard Class 4 4-6-0 No 75025, with a work-stained smokebox, rests over one of the pits at the front of Exmouth Junction shed with Ivatt Class 2 2-6-2T No 41307 behind and 'Battle of Britain' class 4-6-2 No 34063 *229 Squadron* alongside on 6 December 1964. *Maurice Dart*

Right:
Basking in the winter sun outside Exmouth Junction shed on 22 December 1963 is Rebuilt 'Merchant Navy' class 4-6-2 No 35013 *Blue Funnel* and several 'West Country' and 'Battle of Britain' class 4-6-2s including Nos 34076 *41 Squadron* and 34106 *Lydford*. *Maurice Dart*

Below left:
'Z' class 0-8-0T No 30950 shunts some wagons in the small yard which adjoined Exmouth Junction shed on 5 July 1961. *R. C. Riley*

Below right:
In ex-works condition, Adams Radial '0415' class 4-4-2T No 30582 is to the fore in the yard at Exmouth Junction shed on 15 July 1960. Among the locomotives in the background are 'West Country' class 4-6-2 No 34063 *229 Squadron* and 'S15' class 4-6-0 No 30826 from Salisbury shed. *R. C. Riley*

Above:
'H15' class 4-6-0 No 30333 from Salisbury shed is on a siding at the side of Exmouth Junction shed as a Bulleid Pacific reverses off the coaling line on 4 April 1958. *Maurice Dart/The Transport Treasury*

Below:
On the ash road at Exmouth Junction shed awaiting coaling are two 'Merchant Navy' class locomotives, with a 'West Country' class in between them, all being 4-6-2s. The locomotive nearest the camera in this 8 July 1949 view is No 35024 *East Asiatic Company* which had worked down from Waterloo on the 'Atlantic Coast Express'. *Maurice Dart collection*

Above:
'M7' class 0-4-4T No 30046 at Seaton with the train to Seaton Junction, showing the one-road locomotive shed on the left in June 1959. *Harry Cowan*

Seaton

The small shed here was alongside the station and accommodated the branch locomotive overnight and at weekends. 'M7' class 0-4-4Ts were the standard power for the branch, and on Monday, 11 June 1962 the locomotive was No 30048.

Exmouth

The shed was adjacent to the landward side of the station and barely held two tank locomotives, which could be viewed from the platform and from the parallel road, through the shed's windows.

Sunday, 27 March 1955		**Sunday, 7 April 1963**	
Class O2 0-4-4T	30199	Class 2 2-6-2T	41292, 41322
Class 2 2-6-2T	41314	Class 4 2-6-4T	80038
Class 3 2-6-2T	82018		

Broad Clyst Permanent Way Depot

There was no shed building here; the locomotive stood on one of the depot sidings on the up side of the main lines. On 31 August 1958, 4-wheel petrol locomotive No 49S was present, which was shortly replaced by Ruston & Hornsby 4-wheel diesel No DS1169.

Right:
Seaton on 5 July 1949, with the tiny locomotive shed on the left with its water tank. The train to Seaton Junction is at the platform in the charge of Adams '0415' class 'Radial' 4-4-2T No 3488, which under the BR renumbering scheme became 30583. *Maurice Dart collection*

Below left:
Despite the fact that there was no shed provided, a locomotive was based at Broad Clyst Permanent Way Depot to deal with the shunting at that location. It was reputedly a home-made machine, numbered 49S, which, at a quick glance, resembled a small covered van and is seen here in the yard with an equally archaic-looking coach which was in use as a tool van on 31 August 1958. *Maurice Dart/The Transport Treasury*

Below right:
The small shed at Exmouth, with its water tank unusually above the office at the rear, has a pair of Ivatt Class 2 2-6-2Ts on shed, one of which is No 41320, in August 1962. *Author's collection*

Okehampton

This was a single-road sub-shed to Exmouth Junction which could accommodate two tender locomotives. It adjoined the north end of the station which was high above the town, in a very exposed position. It was normally frequented by 'T9s' and 'Ns', which latterly were displaced by BR Standard 4-6-0s and 2-6-4Ts. I went around the shed 16 times.

Saturday, 26 November 1955

Class N 2-6-0	31844/46 (both 72A)
Class T9 4-4-0	30710 (72A)

Sunday, 6 September 1964

Class 4 2-6-4T	80041/59/64 (all 83D)

Shed Codes

72A and 83D, both Exmouth Junction

Left:
Okehampton shed is in the right background and the coaling stage is behind 'T9' class 4-4-0 No 30717 from Exmouth Junction shed which is on the turntable. 14 July 1959. *R. C. Riley*

Above left:
The moorland shed at Okehampton, with the coaling stage on the left, and 'T9' class 4-4-0 No 30710 and 'N' class 2-6-0 No 31849 in the yard on 15 September 1956. Peeping out of the shed is 'West Country' class 4-6-2 No 34034 *Honiton*. The high signal with a repeater arm at the top was an aid to sighting from an up train approaching the station.
Stephenson Locomotive Society

Above right:
'T9' class 4-4-0 No 30710 stands outside Okehampton shed on 26 November 1955 in heavy rain, typical of this Dartmoor town. It was a regular locomotive at this location for many years. *Maurice Dart/The Transport Treasury*

Right:
On another very wet day in early 1964, BR Standard Class 4 2-6-4T No 80037 sits on the turntable at Okehampton shed. Concrete products from the works at Exmouth Junction are much in evidence in this scene. *Mike Daly*

Meldon Quarry

There was a small shed adjacent to the main line which accommodated the quarry shunting loco. It was never necessary to visit the shed as any locomotive therein could be identified from a passing train.

Locomotives which I observed at the quarry included 'T' class 0-6-0T No 500S, which was withdrawn in November 1949 but lingered on, dumped at the end of a siding at the north end of the quarry, for several months. Replacements were 'G6' class 0-6-0T No DS3152, withdrawn August 1960; 'G6' No DS682, withdrawn December 1962, followed by 'USA' class 0-6-0T No DS234. If the normal locomotive was under repair the replacement on loan was usually 'O2' class 0-4-4T No 30199 or 30232. From November 1966, Class 08 diesel shunters took over duties here.

Right:
Resting inside the shed at Meldon Quarry is 'G6' class 0-6-0T No DS3152, which was previously No 30272. The ballast storage and loading hoppers are on the left in this 3 October 1959 view. *Maurice Dart/The Transport Treasury*

Bude

The single-road shed was situated alongside the lines entering the station and could hold one tank loco, usually overnight. It was unoccupied each time I went there.

Right:
Bude shed is seen on 21 November 1964, with the station in the background, and BR Standard Class 3 2-6-2T No 82030 being prepared for its return working to Okehampton. *Terry Nicholls*

Far right:
Standing outside the small one-road shed at Bude in the late afternoon sun on 16 June 1962 is 'N' class 2-6-0 No 31406 from Exmouth Junction shed, awaiting its next turn on a train to Okehampton. The water tank is to the left, with the goods shed on the opposite side of the running lines. *R. C. Riley*

NOTICE

Launceston (SR)

This was a single-road shed, located south of the station, behind the goods yard. For many years it was used only to turn and water locomotives, as the ex-GWR shed was used for overnight and weekend stabling. On Saturday 25 June 1955, '4575' class 2-6-2T No 5531 worked the 3.10pm Plymouth to Launceston train. It came off the train in the SR station and ran through the shed to the SR turntable, before and after turning. The building appeared increasingly more decrepit each time I visited it.

Above right:
Class 4575 2-6-2T No 5531 had worked to Launceston on the 3.10pm from Plymouth North Road on 25 June 1955. On arrival, it detached from the train and went to the SR shed to be turned on the table, which necessitated running through the shed. *Maurice Dart/The Transport Treasury*

Above:
Class 8750 0-6-0PT No 4656 is passing the decrepit ex-SR shed at Launceston, with the ex-SR goods shed on the left, on 25 September 1961. The twin stations are seen to the left of the locomotive with the ex-GWR yard over to the right. *R. S. Carpenter Photos*

Right:
'4575' class 2-6-2T No 5541 has worked a train from Plymouth to Launceston and has come to the ex-SR shed to turn. The ramshackle remains of the shed are behind the locomotive whilst the ex-GWR shed was to the left on the opposite side of the running lines on 2 May 1961.
R. C. Riley

Barnstaple Junction — BPL/72E/83F from 9/9/63

The two-road shed was east of the goods shed and the front of the yard was visible from the station platform. Access to the shed was by a short walk from the station, and I was never refused entry.

Ex-SR types were gradually displaced by Ivatt Class 2 2-6-2Ts and it was normal to find an ex-GWR locomotive present after that company's shed at Victoria Road had closed in January 1951. I went around this shed four times.

Saturday, 21 June 1958

Class M7 0-4-4T	30247/51/52/53/54/56, 30671
Class N 2-6-0	31831/32/38/42 (all 72A)
Class WC/BB 4-6-2	34035/74 (both 72A)
Class 4300 2-6-0	7304 (83B)
Class 2 2-6-2T	41295, 41314

Monday, 3 June 1963

Class N 2-6-0	31818 (72A)
Class 4300 2-6-0	7326 (83B)
Class 2 2-6-2T	41214/16/90/97/98, 41310

Shed Codes

72A Exmouth Junction; 83B Taunton

Above right:
While working portions of the route taken by the 'Exmoor Ranger' railtour, '2251' class 0-6-0 No 3205 called in at the closed Barnstaple Junction shed and took water, as fortunately the facilities there were still workable on 27 March 1965. *Maurice Dart*

Lower right:
Barnstaple Junction shed building was in a woebegone state when this photograph was taken on a Whit Monday, 3 June 1963. Locomotives visible are Ivatt Class 2 2-6-2Ts Nos 41297, 41290, 41298, 41310 and 41216 (No 41214 was also on shed), and in the distance, '4300' class 2-6-0 No 7326 and 'N' class 2-6-0 No 31818. *Maurice Dart*

Above:
'M7' class 0-4-4T No 30670, by the coaling stage at Barnstaple Junction shed on 23 August 1962.
Pamlin Prints/Maurice Dart collection

Above right:
Seen in the yard at Barnstaple Junction shed are Ivatt Class 2 2-6-2T No 41314 by the coaling stage, 'M7' class 0-4-4T No 30256, and another Ivatt tank, No 41295, right, on 21 June 1958.
Maurice Dart

Right:
In front of the shed at Barnstaple Junction are 'M7' class 0-4-4T No 30256 and Ivatt Class 2 2-6-2T No 41297 on 19 July 1958.
The Transport Treasury

Above:
The shed at Barnstaple Junction became rather decrepit as time passed. Standing outside are Ivatt Class 2 2-6-2T No 41224 and 'Battle of Britain' class 4-6-2 No 34070 *Manston*, from Exmouth Junction shed, with another Ivatt tank lurking inside in the summer of 1963. *A. Scarsbrook/Initial Photographics*

BRITISH
RAILWAYS

Left:
With the decrepit shed in the background, '4300' class 2-6-0 No 6363 from Taunton shed stands in the yard at Barnstaple Junction shed with, in the distance, what appears to be a 'N' class 2-6-0, on 20 July 1964. *R. C. Riley*

Ilfracombe

The small, one-road shed here would accommodate one locomotive overnight or between turns. It was just south of the station and was easily viewed from the road which ran parallel to the railway.

Sunday, 22 June 1958
The shed was empty, but 'N' class 2-6-0 No 31842 (72A) had emerged to act as banker.

Monday, 3 June 1963
Class N 2-6-0 31840 (72A)

Upper right:
Being turned on the table at the rear of Ilfracombe shed on 8 August 1952 is 'West Country' class 4-6-2 No 34001 *Exeter*. The coaling stage is to the right of the shed and the station is just visible in the upper left-hand corner.
R. J. Leonard/Maurice Dart collection

Lower right:
The small sub-shed at Torrington is seen on 17 April 1954, with 'E1/R' class 0-6-2T No 32095 standing outside. *B. K. B. Green/Initial Photographics*

Torrington

The shed was behind the west side of the station, somewhat hidden from view. It could hold a couple of tank locomotives, usually overnight.

Saturday, 21 June 1958
Class M7 0-4-4T 30255 (72E)

Shed Codes
72A Exmouth Junction; 72E Barnstaple Junction

72D Plymouth Friary — PLY/72D/83H from 1/2/58

This was a fairly long, three-road shed with a small yard at each end and a hoist beside the building. The coaling stage was quite small. A 15-minute walk from the station took you to the entrance gate from where a boarded crossing led to the shed. I was never refused entry and only recall seeing the shed foreman if I went to his office to ask permission to go around or to seek information. The last foreman was Jimmy Trigger who was always very helpful.

Friary could spring surprises at times with the arrival of a fresh locomotive type or a replacement for one away at works. A good example of the latter occurred on 3 March 1957 when 'B4' class 0-4-0T No 30082 (71A) was on shed and remained for three months while sister locomotive No 30102 was away. The diminutive 'B4' shunting tanks remained here until they were replaced by 204hp diesel shunters. The ex-SR types were gradually succeeded by Ivatt and BR Standard tanks. I went around the shed at least 25 times, but usually only if I knew there was a fresh locomotive present.

Friday, 25 December 1953

Class B4 0-4-0T	30088/94, 30102
Class E1/R 0-6-2T	32094/95
Class M7 0-4-4T	30034/35/37/39/40
Class O2 0-4-4T	30183/92, 30236
Class N 2-6-0	31833 (72A)
Class WC/BB 4-6-2	34031/32/57/60 (all 72A), 34035/36/37/38
PDSWJ 0-6-2T	30757/58

Sunday, 31 March 1963

Class N 2-6-0	31845 (72A)
Class WC/BB 4-6-2	34065/72/81, 34110 (all 72A)
Class 2 2-6-2T	41206 (72A), 41275/95 (both 72F), 41315/17

Shed Codes

71A Eastleigh; 72A Exmouth Junction; 72F Wadebridge

Upper right:
The south end of Plymouth Friary shed with 'N' class 2-6-0 No 31871 inside and 'T1' class 0-4-4T No 7 (not yet not renumbered in the BR 30,000 series) just outside, on 17 April 1949. *B. K. B. Green/Initial Photographics*

Lower right:
Outside the south end of Plymouth Friary are 'B4' class 0-4-0Ts Nos 30083 and 30102 being prepared to go off shed in the morning, June 1957.
Denis Richards

Right:
A line of locomotives outside the north end of Plymouth Friary shed comprises Drewry 0-6-0D No 11225, 'M7' class 0-4-4T No 30034, 'O2' class 0-4-4T No 30192 and M7 No 30036, c1959. *D. I. D. Loveday/Maurice Dart collection*

Below left:
In the yard at the south end of Plymouth Friary shed in October 1952 are ex-PD&SWJR 0-6-2T No 30758 *Lord St. Levan* and 'M7' class 0-4-4T No 30037. *Maurice Dart collection*

Below right:
Newcomers to the Plymouth area at this time were the 'E1/R' class 0-6-2Ts, one of which, No 32094, is seen outside the north end of Plymouth Friary shed in October 1952. *Maurice Dart collection*

Left:
Alongside the shed at Plymouth Friary, standing on the Hoist road, are 'B4' class 0-4-0T No 30088 and '02' class 0-4-4T No 30193 on 4 July 1957.*R. C. Riley*

Below left:
At Plymouth Friary shed, 'B4' class 0-4-0T No 30089 awaits the next turn at the coaling stage while a Bulleid Light Pacific has its tender supply replenished in August 1957. *Denis Richards*

Below right:
'West Country' class 4-6-2 No 34002 *Salisbury* stands alongside a line of locomotives in Plymouth Friary shed: Ivatt Class 2 2-6-2T No 41317, an 'M7' class 0-4-4T, another Ivatt 2-6-2T, an 'O2' class 0-4-4T and a Bulleid Light Pacific on 13 July 1958. *The Transport Treasury*

Callington

The shed was in the station yard and contained two dead-end roads, each of which could hold one tank locomotive. Normally, one locomotive was kept there overnight and at weekends.

Above:
Ivatt Class 2 2-6-2T No 41317 from Plymouth Friary shed quietly smokes outside the shed at Callington with its crew on board, ready to back out and run into the station to work a train to Bere Alston, on 28 August 1961.
R. C. Riley

Left:
Outside the small shed at Callington in June 1961 is 'O2' class 0-4-4T No 30183 which has replenished its coal supply from the adjacent wagons and is ready to work the next service to Bere Alston.
Harry Cowan

Lower left:
'West Country' class 4-6-2 No 34019 *Bideford* rests by the entrance to the yard at Wadebridge shed on 9 June 1949. These locomotives had to go on to Padstow to be turned.
R. J. Buckley/Initial Photographics

72F Wadebridge — WAD/72F/84E from 9/9/63

The two-road shed was alongside the station and to reach it, one walked from the station, over the level crossing and along a footpath past the turntable. Mr Brown was the last foreman, who was always very helpful, but I rarely saw him as I usually visited during the evening or on a Sunday. I went around the shed only 11 times as it was not normally necessary to do so.

For many years, the famous Beattie well tanks were the attraction of a visit here, until replaced by ex-GWR '1366' class outside-cylinder 0-6-0PTs and likewise, ex-SR 'O2s' were replaced by ex-GWR 0-6-0PTs, which were themselves displaced by Ivatt tanks.

Sunday, 6 May 1956	
Class 0298 2-4-0T	30585/86/87
Class N 2-6-0	31836 (72A)
Class O2 0-4-4T	30200/36
Class T9 4-4-0	30709 (72A)
Class U 2-6-0	31610 (72C)
Class WC 4-6-2	34004 (72A)

Sunday, 17 June 1962	
Class 0298 2-4-0WT	30585/86/87
Class 1366 0-6-0PT	1368
Class 8750 0-6-0PT	4666
Class 2 2-6-2T	41272 (72A)

Shed Codes
72A Exmouth Junction;
72C Yeovil Town

Above:
Lined up in front of the shed at Wadebridge are, left to right, 'N' class 2-6-0s Nos 31844, 31846 and 31845, c1953. *Maurice Dart collection*

Right:
A Saturday afternoon at Wadebridge finds 'N' class 2-6-0 No 31840, left, outside the shed, while inside are 'O2' class 0-4-4T No 30236 and '0298' class 2-4-0WTs Nos 30586 and 30585 on 31 May 1958. *Maurice Dart*

Above:
Standing in staggered formation at the front of the yard at Wadebridge shed on 21 June 1962 are Beattie '0298' class 2-4-0WTs Nos 30587, 30586 and 30585. This trio had survived here for very many years to work trains over the branch line to Wenford Bridge but were on the point of being replaced by a trio of ex-GWR '1366' class 0-6-0PTs. *R. C. Riley*

Right:
Beattie '0298' class 2-4-0WT No 30585 stands alongside '1366' class 0-6-0PT No 1368 near the coal stage in the yard, in front of the shed at Wadebridge, on 22 June 1962. *R. C. Riley*

Below left:
On 27 April 1963 one of the replacements for the famous Beattie well tanks stands inside the shed at Wadebridge in the form of '1366' class 0-6-0PT No 1368, sporting its freshly applied 72F shedplate. *Maurice Dart*

Below right:
'N' class 2-6-0 No 31406, from Exmouth Junction shed, stands under the coaling stage at Wadebridge shed with steam issuing from its front cocks on 27 April 1963. *Maurice Dart*

Left:
BR Standard Class 4 2-6-4T No 80039 moves off the shed at Wadebridge, past the building with the coaling stage beyond, on the right, c1964. *Rex Conway collection/Maurice Dart collection*

Left:
The back end of Wadebridge shed, viewed from behind the turntable, with a pair of 'T9' class 4-4-0s, Nos 30717 and 30729, and an 'N' class 2-6-0 visible in between. On the left is the cycle shed, c1960. *Maurice Dart collection*

Right:
A railwayman leans on the bar and exerts maximum effort as he turns 'N' class 2-6-0 No 31406 on the turntable at Wadebridge shed, c1962. *Mike Daly*

Padstow

There was no locomotive shed here, but watering facilities and a 70ft-diameter turntable were provided, this latter item being used to turn Bulleid Pacifics which had worked in.

Below:
The turntable at Wadebridge shed was too short to handle the Bulleid Light Pacifics so they had to run to Padstow to be turned, as has 'West Country' class 4-6-2 No 34038 *Lynton*, seen in the late 1950s. *Hugh Davies Photographs*

Exeter EXE/83C

The shed was visible from St Davids station, from where it was accessed by a boarded crossing, but, as this crossed many lines, enthusiasts were not permitted to use it. By going over Red Cow Crossing at the up end of the station you could continue over the goods lines and follow a path to reach the four-road shed, to which a door in the side gave access. As this was remote from the shed office it was possible to go around without asking permission, but in later years we always saw the foreman first and were never refused entry.

A one-road lifting shop was hidden behind the west side of the shed. Most locomotives in the yard could be identified from the station, including a couple which usually stood by the pump house. From the late 1950s, locomotives were stored behind the coaling stage and c1964, after the shed had closed to steam traction, withdrawn locomotives, including some ex-SR types, were stored in the now roofless shed in company with diesel-hydraulics. In total, I visited the shed 21 times and only once had a permit.

Sunday, 24 May 1953

Class 1000 4-6-0	1007 (82A)
Class 1400 0-4-2T	1405/29/40/51/68/69
Class 2251 0-6-0	2230
Class 4073 4-6-0	4079 (84A), 5003
Class 4300 2-6-0	5321
Class 4575 2-6-2T	5557 (83A)
Class 4900 4-6-0	4932
Class 5101 2-6-2T	4176
Class 5700 0-6-0PT	5760, 7716/61
Class 6959 4-6-0	6986 (82A)
Class 8750 0-6-0PT	3603/06/77, 3794, 9765
Class 9400 0-6-0PT	8456, 9439

Shed Codes
82A Bath Road, Bristol
83A Newton Abbot
84A Wolverhampton (Stafford Road)

Right:
'Castle' class 4-6-0 No 4037 *The South Wales Borderers*, fitted with Hawksworth flush-sided tender, stands in the yard at Exeter shed on 2 September 1962.
Mike Daly

Above:
An overview of Exeter GWR shed on 23 September 1962, showing the coaling facility on the left, the shed yard with the four-road shed building in the background, to the left of which is the one-road locomotive 'Factory'. The locomotives visible include 'Halls' and a '5101' class 2-6-2T. *R. C. Riley*

Below left:
The four-road locomotive shed at Exeter was situated behind St Davids station. In front of the shed are '5101' class 2-6-2T No 4117 and '8750' class 0-6-0PTs Nos 9629 and 3603. The shed offices are on the left of the building in this 4 April 1958 view. *Denis Richards*

Below right:
The coaling line at Exeter shed. A 'Grange' class 4-6-0 has just been coaled and '9400' class 0-6-0PT No 9439 awaits its turn by the coaling stage, which holds wagons containing coal, on 12 July 1958. *The Transport Treasury*

Sunday, 11 October 1959

Class 1000 4-6-0	1007/23
Class 1400 0-4-2T	1440/51/52/68/71
Class 2251 0-6-0	2244 (82B)
Class 4073 4-6-0	5075
Class 4300 2-6-0	6337 (83B), 6360 (83A), 7311
Class 4575 2-6-2T	5521/24
Class 4900 4-6-0	4944, 5975, 6965
Class 5101 2-6-2T	4117/36
Class 5400 0-6-0PT	5412
Class 5700 0-6-0PT	7716
Class 6400 0-6-0PT	6402/14 (Wdn), 6406 (83D).
Class 8750 0-6-0PT	9629, 9765
Class 9400 0-6-0PT	9497
Class 8F 2-8-0	48404 (82B)
Class WD 2-8-0	90323 (86C)
Diesel 0-6-0	D3521

Shed Codes

82B St Philip's Marsh, Bristol; 83A Newton Abbot; 83B Taunton; 83D Laira, Plymouth; ; 86C Cardiff Canton; Wdn Withdrawn

Right:
There was a one-road 'Factory' at Exeter shed which, on this occasion on 22 March 1959, appears to be occupied by an open wagon with 'Hall' class 4-6-0 No 4927 *Farnborough Hall* from Bath Road shed outside. A far rarer visitor is '2884' class 2-8-0 No 3828 from Croes Newydd shed at Wrexham, standing between the 'Factory' and the sand house. *Maurice Dart/ The Transport Treasury*

Below left:
A view from the side door, showing the back end of Exeter shed with 'Hall' class 4-6-0 No 4944 *Middleton Hall* and '1400' class 0-4-2T No 1471 present, on 22 March 1959. *Maurice Dart/The Transport Treasury*

Below right:
Class 4300 2-6-0 No 7316 rests on the turntable at Exeter shed, with the top of the coaling stage visible above the tender, on 22 March 1959. *Mike Daly*

Left:
After Exeter shed closed to steam in October 1963, it was used to store withdrawn steam locomotives which had been allocated there and at Exmouth Junction, as well as stabling diesels. In the now roofless shed stands 'N' class 2-6-0 No 31842 in company with another 'N', right, No 31834, on 26 June 1964. *Maurice Dart*

Below:
A 20 September 1960 panorama of Exeter shed, showing, from left to right, the 'Factory' (lifting shop), the shed offices and the running shed. Among the locomotives on shed is '8750' class 0-6-0PT No 3794.
Maurice Dart collection

Above:
A 23 June 1962 panoramic view of the shed and yard at Exeter GWR, with many locomotives visible, including 4-6-0s, 0-6-0PTs and 0-4-2Ts. A Type 2 diesel-hydraulic is adjacent to the lifting shop, and the goods shed and St Davids station are to the right, with, in the far distance, the start of Riverside yard.
The photographer was presumably on the top of the water tank which was situated above the pump house. *R. C. Riley*

Left:
The yard at Exeter shed on 16 September 1961, with '1400' class 0-4-2Ts Nos 1420, 1471 and 1434 (on loan from Laira) in front of the coaling line. Note the unusual crossover leading to the turntable. *Maurice Dart/The Transport Treasury*

Left:
After closure, the shed at Exeter lost its roof and was used to store withdrawn locomotives such as 'Battle of Britain' class 4-6-2 No 34075 *264 Squadron* and 'N' class 2-6-0 No 31821, both previously shedded at Exmouth Junction, seen on 26 June 1964. *Maurice Dart/The Transport Treasury*

Right:
The withdrawn locomotives in the roofless shed at Exeter seen here on 26 June 1964 are 'N' class 2-6-0 No 31842, and '2251' class 0-6-0s Nos 2214 and 3205, nearest the camera. *Maurice Dart*

Below:
Withdrawn ex-SR Exmouth Junction shed locomotives are stored c1963 in the yard at Exeter shed, behind the coaling stage, included 'N' class 2-6-0 No 31409 and '700' class 0-6-0 No 30700, which had been used for snowplough duties on the line to Okehampton and Plymouth.
Maurice Dart collection

Above:
Recently ex works, '5101' class 2-6-2T No 4117 stands in the yard at Exeter shed on 16 July 1958. *R. C. Riley*

Tiverton Junction

This one-road shed was beside the branch to Tiverton, just as it curved away from the junction station. A pair of '1400' class 0-4-2Ts were sub-shedded here from Exeter to work the two branches, only using the shed overnight and at weekends.

Above:
The locomotive shed at Tiverton Junction, seen from behind the station platform with the coaling stage to the left together with the obligatory coal wagon standing on the siding behind it, on 24 September 1961. Usually, it was only overnight when an incumbent locomotive could be found in the shed. The branch line to Tiverton swings off to the right past the flat wagons loaded with containers. *R. S. Carpenter Photos*

Right:
In the early 1950s Class 1400 0-4-2T No 1469 propels its auto-train out of Tiverton Junction towards Tiverton, soon passing the locomotive shed visible on the left. *R. E. Toop/Maurice Dart collection*

Left:
BR Standard Class 5 4-6-0 No 73133, fitted with Caprotti valve gear, from Shrewsbury shed, was quite a rare visitor to Newton Abbot shed where it waits in the yard, ready to take up its duty. Within a few weeks of this August 1958 picture this locomotive was transferred to Patricroft shed, Manchester. *Mike Daly*

Right:
The yard at the front of Newton Abbot shed is seen in June 1954 with the water tank and coaling stage roof to the left. Locomotives visible include 'Castle' class 4-6-0 No 7023 *Penrice Castle* from Canton shed, Cardiff, '5101' class 2-6-2T No 4127 from Birkenhead shed (probably for works), a 'Hall' class 4-6-0, a '5700' class 0-6-0PT, an '8750' class 0-6-0PT, '4500' class 2-6-2T No 4547, and '4300' class 2-6-0 No 5362. *Rail Archive Stephenson*

Newton Abbot NA/83A

This was a very busy and important six-road long shed which was unusual in having the coaling-stage lines, turntable and part of its yard on a lower level. The situation was made even more interesting by the presence of a rather important locomotive works which backed on to the rear of the shed. The shed and the works were separate entities, but at times when down in the yard, it was difficult to decide which section one was actually in. On one occasion, when I had a permit for the shed, I had reached the north end of the coaling line and thought I would go a little further to reach a small porch on the side of the works from which most of the locomotives inside could be identified. Just as I had reached it a group of men in suits came around from the front of the works and one of them, whom I assumed to be the Divisional Locomotive Superintendent, Mr Christison, accosted me vigorously, whereupon I showed him my permit, but to no avail, and was told I should not be in that area. However, one of the others intervened and overruled him and gave me permission to go inside the works, which amazed me, and I heard the other person say: 'Oh, all right Mr Smeddle.' I smiled to myself, as I had read his name on various works' permits over the years, and I thanked him very much.

On another occasion, when I had permits to visit the works and the shed in that order, I was conducted through the complex of workshops and offices which segregated them, in order to reach the shed. Mr Christison was extremely strict so it was impossible to gain entry without a permit, but I did manage it once with a great deal of luck. Having been around on organised visits several times I knew the layout, so one weekend evening I decided to go up the entrance drive to the works and walk down past the coaling stage from where steps led up to the top yard and shed. As I approached the coaling stage I espied the foreman sitting in the sun talking to one of the shedmen, and he saw me coming. He asked me how I had entered, but before I could answer he remarked that he had not seen me cross the tracks from the station and guessed what I had done. Then, to my utter surprise, he said I could carry on and have a good look around.

The correct entrance to the shed was through a doorway in a wall which faced the window in the foreman's office. Normally a face appeared at the window and you were told to leave. I went to the shed office one weekday in May 1959 and was immediately told I should not be in there, but I informed the foreman that I only wished to enquire where newly transferred No 5573 would be. Whereupon, I was informed with much laughter that I would have to go down to Penzance to see it as it had gone there on loan a few days earlier. The laughter increased considerably when I remarked that I had come up from St Austell to Plymouth the previous evening. So we parted company quite affably.

I went around the shed 10 times and the works six times, but it was really like Fort Knox for visiting. Locomotives from all parts of the ex-GWR system could be seen here at times, either awaiting attention or ex works, which made a visit extremely interesting.

In the early 1950s, three 'Dukedog' 4-4-0s were transferred here on loan from Didcot and Swindon, but by the time I obtained a permit to visit the depot two of them had gone back.

Monday, 26 November 1951	
Shed	
Class 1400 0-4-2T	1466
Class 1600 0-6-0PT	1608
Class 2800 2-8-0	2875
Class 4073 4-6-0	5071, 7000
Class 4500 2-6-2T	4547
Class 4575 2-6-2T	4582, 5505, 5572 (82A)
Class 5101 2-6-2T	4176 (83C), 5113/40/42/57
Class 8750 0-6-0PT	9668
Class 7200 2-8-2T	7236/40/50
Class 7400 0-6-0PT	7427, 7442 (81B)
Class 7800 4-6-0	7805, 7806 (83E)
Class 9000 4-4-0	9018 (82C)

Monday, 26 November 1951	
Works	
Class 1000 4-6-0	1024 (83D)
Class 1361 0-6-0ST	1362 (Works pilot)
Class 1400 0-4-2T	1468 (83C)
Class 2021 0-6-0PT	2088 (83C)
Class 2800 2-8-0	2869
Class 4500 2-6-2T	4558 (81F)
Class 4900 4-6-0	4937 (87G), 4967, 6903 (both 82B)
Class 5600 0-6-2T	5625 (86E)
Class 5700 0-6-0PT	7761 (83C), 7777 (81D)
Class 6800 4-6-0	6814, 6874 (86A)
Class 8750 0-6-0PT	3705 (83E)
Class 9400 0-6-0PT	9440

Shed Codes

81B Slough; 81D Reading; 81F Oxford; 82A Bath Road, Bristol; 82B St Philips Marsh, Bristol; 82C Swindon; 83C Exeter; 83D Laira; 83E St Blazey; 86A Newport (Ebbw Junction); 87E Severn Tunnel Junction; 87G Carmarthem

Above:
On 15 July 1959 Class 1400 0-4-2T No 1452 hauls ex-works, St Philip's Marsh-allocated '8750' class 0-6-0PT No 3692 past the coaling line at Newton Abbot shed. The sidings between the shed and the station contain the breakdown train and other rolling stock, while to the far left can he seen the framework of one of the buildings for servicing diesels. *R. C. Riley*

Above:
Three 'Hall' class 4-6-0s wait in line at the west end of Newton Abbot shed yard while a '5101' class 2-6-2T is in the background being coaled and No 4178 of the same class waits at the station with a short local train for the Torbay line, on 19 July 1959. *R. C. Riley*

Right:
A weather vane depicting a GWR broad-gauge 4-2-2, complete with footplate crew, stands proudly aloft the roof at the east end of Newton Abbot Locomotive Works on 15 July 1961, leaving no doubt as to the identity of the works' original owners. *R. C. Riley*

Saturday, 23 November 1957
Shed

Class 1000 4-6-0	1002/06 (both 83G), 1028 (82A)
Class 1400 0-4-2T	1452 (87J)
Class 1600 0-6-0PT	1608
Class 2800 2-8-0	2846
Class 2884 2-8-0	3834 (83C), 3841, 3844 (86E)
Class 4073 4-6-0	7000
Class 4200 2-8-0T	4247 (83E)
Class 4575 2-6-2T	5533
Class 4900 4-6-0	4949 (83B), 4950 (83G), 4967, 4989 (81D), 5920, 6933
Class 5101 2-6-2T	4133 (82F), 4109/50/78, 5108/53/68/78/83/95/96
Class 6800 4-6-0	6855/73 (both 83D)
Class 7400 0-6-0PT	7427/45
Class 7800 4-6-0	7813
Class 8750 0-6-0PT	3600, 3677 (83C), 9633/78
Class 9400 0-6-0PT	9487
Class 8F 2-8-0	48461 (82B)

Saturday, 23 November 1957
Works

Class 1361 0-6-0ST	1364 (83D)
Class 1400 0-4-2T	1444 (81D), 1466/72
Class 1600 0-6-0PT	1624 (83E)
Class 2251 0-6-0	2230 (83B)
Class 2800 2-8-0	2881
Class 4073 4-6-0	5005, 5072 (83D)
Class 4500 2-6-2T	4555 (82D)
Class 4575 2-6-2T	4577 (82A) (badly damaged)
Class 4900 4-6-0	6941 (83D)
Class 5101 2-6-2T	5150/58
Class 5400 0-6-0PT	5420 (81C)
Class 5700 0-6-0PT	7749 (82B)
Class 6800 4-6-0	6800 (83G)
Class 8750 0-6-0PT	4655 (82B), 9795 (82C)
Class 9400 0-6-0PT	8421/86 (both 83F)
Ex-TVR 0-6-2T	361 (boiler unit only)

Shed Codes

81B Slough; 81C Southall; 81D Reading; 81F Oxford; 82A Bath Road, Bristol; 82B St Philip's Marsh, Bristol; 82C Swindon; 82D Westbury; 82F Weymouth; 83B Taunton; 83C Exeter; 83D Laira, Plymouth; 83E St Blazey; 83F Truro; 83G Penzance; 86E Severn Tunnel Junction; 87G Carmarthen; 87J Goodwick, Fishguard

Left:
The front yard at Newton Abbot shed shown in June 1960 after some changes had taken place. The water tank, which was on the left, has disappeared and a new office block has replaced the old structure. The line-up of locomotives comprises ex-LMS '8F' class 2-8-0 No 48459 from St Philip's Marsh shed, Bristol, '5101' class 2-6-2Ts Nos 5158, 4105 and 5164, and 'County' class 4-6-0 No 1016 *County of Hants*.
P. H. Groom/Maurice Dart collection

Below left:
In parts of the yard, opposite the station at Newton Abbot, it was difficult to decide if one was actually in the shed or works area. In front of the locomotive works (visible in the background in this photograph taken on 10 February 1957) was the weighing shed, through which one line passed, but which rarely seemed to contain any locomotives or rolling stock. Outside this building are 0-6-0PTs '1600' class No 1608 and '8750' class No 9678. *Brian Mennie/Maurice Dart collection*

Above right:
At Newton Abbot, one road led from the front of the shed along the east side of the locomotive works building to reach some sidings. 'Castle' class 4-6-0 No 4037 *The South Wales Borderers* is at the eastern end of the works, with one wagon, on 29 August 1957. *Maurice Dart collection*

Below right:
1361 'class' 0-6-0ST No 1362 acted as works/shed pilot at Newton Abbot and is moving a dead '4575' class 2-6-2T over one of the turntables as 'Manor' class 4-6-0 No 7804 *Baydon Manor* from Laira shed passes the power station on a down train on 5 June 1949. *B. K. B. Green/Initial Photographics*

Moretonhampstead, Ashburton and Kingsbridge

Each of these was a small, one-road shed to accommodate the branch locomotive overnight and at weekends. Kingsbridge was adjacent to the station platform, while the others were situated in their respective station yards. The first two usually housed one '1400' class 0-4-2T, but Kingsbridge would be host to a Small Prairie tank.

Left:
Ashburton shed, which could accommodate one locomotive, is seen from the adjacent road, with its doors closed. Was there an 0-4-2T lurking inside? The raised smoke vents are prominent above the roof in this June 1954 photograph. *Rail Archive Stephenson*

Below left:
An overall view of Kingsbridge in August 1953 with, from left to right: goods yard sidings; carriage sidings and shed; '4575' class 2-6-2T No 5505 at the platform with a train for Brent, with the station buildings behind it; to the right the one-road locomotive shed occupied by a coal wagon, with the water tank alongside. *Maurice Dart collection*

Below right:
Kingsbridge in the mid-1950s, showing, from left to right, the goods yard; carriage sidings and shed, the station, the locomotive shed and the water tank. *Joe Moss, Maurice Dart collection*

Above:
The 2.15pm auto-train from Newton Abbot has arrived at Moretonhampstead on 7 June 1958 and '1400' class 0-4-2T No 1427 is about to run round to detach a van. The one-road locomotive shed, with its water tank, can be seen beyond the station's overall roof, right, empty as usual during daytime. *Peter Gray*

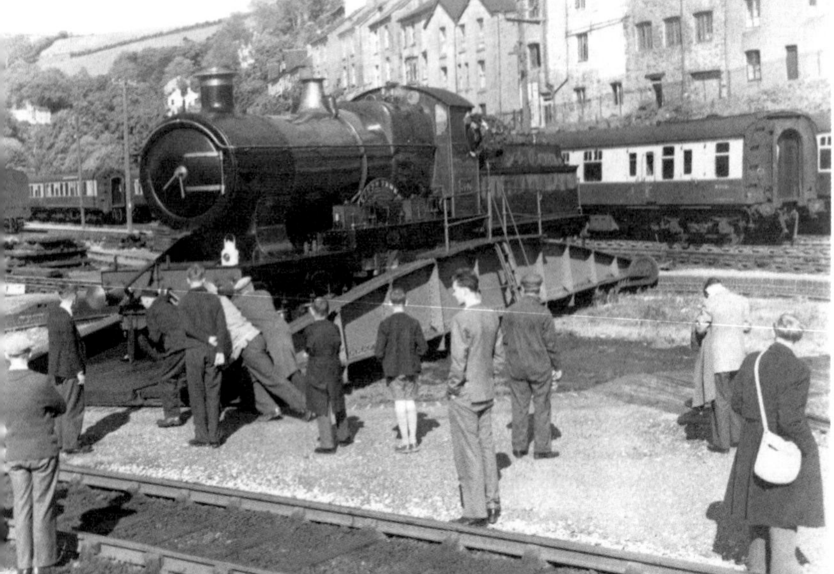

Above:
There was no locomotive shed at Kingswear but a turntable and watering facilities were provided, together with a few stabling sidings. 'Britannia' class 4-6-2 No 70022 *Tornado* from Newton Abbot shed is being turned ready to work a service eastwards on 10 September 1953. *T. G. Wassell/ Hugh Davies Photos*

Left:
After working a special train to Kingswear, preserved 'City' class 4-4-0 No 3440 *City of Truro* ran to Newton Abbot shed for servicing, but ran back to Kingswear to be turned before working the return service. The author is seen bottom right, contemplating his next photograph, when the locomotive has moved off the turntable, while his friend took this view on 19 May 1957. *Mike Daly*

Kingswear

There was no shed building here, but a turntable and watering facilities were provided.

83D Laira, Plymouth LA/83D/84A from 9/9/63

Having already introduced Laira in the preamble, I can now mention some of its characters and occurrences which took place. Apart from the arrival of a few BR Standard locomotives over the years, the shed maintained a predominantly ex-GWR allocation, albeit with locomotive changes occurring periodically. It could often produce something unusual. On my first ever visit I saw 'USA' 2-8-0 No 3517 in for some attention before going to France, 2-8-0T No 4295 from Landore, Swansea, and 2-8-0 No 2880 from Aberdare, under the hoist. In the late 1940s, '4300' class Moguls from sheds such as Banbury and Neyland were visitors. Harold Luscombe was the shedmaster until steam ended and was very friendly to enthusiasts as also were the running foremen Vince Joiner, Mark Peplar, George Thomas, Fred Manley and Harold Cook, who later became a locomotive inspector. We were allowed to help turn the locomotives for stabling inside the roundhouse and were given virtually the run of the shed. The roundhouse had suffered a few incidents over the years as various indentations and a different section of wall construction bore witness. In 1942, a '7200' class 2-8-2T, which was stabled inside, had a defective regulator which had stuck and not closed properly, the locomotive gradually easing itself forward and into the turntable pit.

Next, during 1944, a 'USA' 2-8-0 was to be moved out on to the turntable and these locomotives were fitted with a 'pull-back' type of regulator which on this locomotive was a bit stiff. The young fireman on board was told to 'give her a bit more' and as he tried to do so, the handle jerked out and the locomotive surged forward across the turntable and ran into a '3150' class 2-6-2T which it pushed out through the shed wall!

In 1948, a couple of enthusiasts (not from Plymouth) boarded a locomotive inside the shed and opened the regulator which caused it to deposit itself in the turntable pit. Mark Peplar was on duty at the time and, quite understandably, from then on would not permit anyone to visit the shed. On principle, we local enthusiasts did not go there when he was on duty as he had always been extremely friendly to us in the past.

Laira provided the locomotives for the branch lines to Launceston via Tavistock and from Yelverton to Princetown, there being a sub-shed at each terminus. In the winter, the latter line was prone to become blocked by snowdrifts and when this occurred Laira would dispatch an engine fitted with a large snowplough and one coach to carry staff and provisions. The locomotive was often one of the older 0-6-0PTs, and Harold Luscombe would accompany it as did Mark Peplar usually. Harold would never permit the train to depart from the shed yard without ensuring there was a full crate of whisky on board as well as food, to sustain the snow clearance workers.

When the BR Standard '9F' 2-10-0s arrived they suffered several minor derailments trying to stable in the two short sidings by the pump house. These sidings had been used at times to stable 'Bulldog' 4-4-0s, then oil-burning 2-8-0s and 4-6-0s, but each was slightly curved and the long-wheelbase 2-10-0s were not able to negotiate them properly.

With the arrival of diesel traction, a screen was erected along the centre of the New shed to separate them from the steam locomotives, but, shortly after, steam was relegated to the yard sidings and the roundhouse.

A surprise came early in 1960 with the arrival of a locomotive of a sub-class never seen here previously, in the form of 0-6-0PT No 6771, to take up stationary boiler duty in the roundhouse. Following the closure of Friary shed in May 1963, ex-SR locomotives, Ivatt tanks and BR Standard types came to Laira for servicing and provided some variety. This continued for a period, even after Laira had officially closed to steam in May 1964.

Above:
Just arrived on the coaling line at Laira shed on the afternoon of Sunday 8 July 1962, is '2884' class 2-8-0 No 3849. The ramp up to the coaling stage became somewhat grass covered as its use decreased with the continuous influx of diesel locomotives. *Maurice Dart/The Transport Treasury*

Above:
Stabled in the sidings alongside the New shed at Laira is 'Castle' class 4-6-0 No 4037 *The South Wales Borderers* from Exeter shed, seen on 5 August 1962.
Mike Daly

Right:
On 5 August 1962 'Castle' class 4-6-0 No 5075 *Wellington* from St Philip's Marsh shed, Bristol, having been coaled, waits its turn to move forward towards the roundhouse at Laira shed from where, after turning, it will probably move out to stable in the New shed area. *Mike Daly*

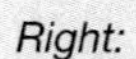

Right:
A 'Hall' class 4-6-0 has been coaled and is awaiting entry to the roundhouse at Laira shed while a 'Castle' class 4-6-0 stands in the siding opposite the coaling stage in August 1962. *Mike Daly*

Above:
The coaling line at Laira shed mid-afternoon on a summer Sunday, 8 July 1962, with, in order, awaiting coaling from the two bays: '2884' class 2-8-0s Nos 3849 and 3854 from St Philip's Marsh shed, Bristol, 'Castle' class 4-6-0 No 7012 *Barry Castle* from Stafford Road shed, Wolverhampton, and a '4500' class 2-6-2T. Items of note are the water tank atop the coaling stage, piles of ash removed from the smokeboxes of locomotives, and a solitary tea-can in the centre of the ash road. *Maurice Dart/The Transport Treasury*

I once obtained a permit to visit Laira, and when I saw the foreman, Fred Manley, he asked why on earth I had bothered to get it. I explained that as I had obtained a permit for almost every other GWR shed, I thought it fitting to have one for my home shed. We both laughed at the idea, but that day I went into parts of the depot such as the stores and the sand house to have a really good look at the parts which I had not normally entered. However, I didn't go into the coaling stage or down the pit into the pump house as the building was locked up.

I suppose I must have visited Laira shed well over 200 times. Now, as I visited the shed so frequently and there were always many locomotives on shed, usually from around the mid-1950s, I only recorded those of interest, so I have no complete lists for Laira from the end of 1954 until just prior to when complete dieselisation occurred.

Friday, 25 December 1953

Class 1000 4-6-0	1006/10
Class 1361 0-6-0ST	1363/64/65
Class 2021 0-6-0PT	2097
Class 2800 2-8-0	2843
Class 2884 2-8-0	2898 (82B), 3805 (86E), 3862
Class 3150 2-6-2T	3186/87
Class 4073 4-6-0	4037, (81A), 4086, 5031 (84A), 5036 (81D), 5056 (81A), 5098
Class 4300 2-6-0	5360/62 (both 83A)
Class 4500 2-6-2T	4524/30/34/42, 4552 (83E)
Class 4575 2-6-2T	4583/90/91, 5531/67
Class 4900 4-6-0	4909/42 (both 82A), 4978, 4999 (82B), 5913, 5926 (83E), 5932/40 (both 81A), 5958 (82B), 5998, 6912, 6914 (82D), 6923 (81D), 7907 (82A)
Class 5101 2-6-2T	5148/75
Class 5700 0-6-0PT	7762, 8709/19
Class 6000 4-6-0	6009 (81A), 6012/14, 6019 (81A), 6022/23/24
Class 6400 0-6-0PT	6406/07/14/19/21
Class 6800 4-6-0	6815 (83B), 6836 (83G), 6838, 6846 (82B), 6869/73
Class 6959 4-6-0	6965, 6967 (82C), 6978, 7905/09, 7916 (83A)
Class 7800 4-6-0	7804, 7808 (82A), 7809/14/15/24
Class 8750 0-6-0PT	3639/75/86, 3787/90, 4653/58/79/93, 9671, 9716
Class 9400 0-6-0PT	8422/25/26, 9433/67
Class 5 4-6-0	73039 (82B)
Class 7P6F 4-6-2	70016, 70018 (81A), 70021/24

Sunday, 31 March 1963

Class 1000 4-6-0	1003/04/15 (all Wdn)
Class 1363 0-6-0ST	1363 (Wdn)
Class 2884 2-8-0	3801/03 (both 86E)
Class 4073 4-6-0	5014 (81A), 5085 (82B), 7022
Class 4300 2-6-0	7316 (Wdn)
Class 4500 2-6-2T	4567/70/74 (all Wdn), 4555
Class 4575 2-6-2T	5544/68 (both Wdn), 4591
Class 4900 4-6-0	4978, 4991(82B), 6966 (81A), 6988 (82A), 7924 (82B)
Class 6400 0-6-0PT	6438 (Wdn)

Shed Codes

81A Old Oak Common; 82A Bath Road, Bristol; 82B St Philip's Marsh, Bristol; 82C Swindon; 82D Westbury; 83A Newton Abbot; 83B Taunton; 83E St Blazey; 83G Penzance; 84A Wolverhampton (Stafford Road); 86E Severn Tunnel Junction; Wdn Withdrawn

Above:
The coaling line at Laira shed on 17 June 1958, during a quiet period with one solitary locomotive awaiting coaling and having the ash removed from its smokebox; a rather unpleasant task, but very necessary. 'Castle' class 4-6-0 No 7031 *Cromwell's Castle* had worked in to North Road, Plymouth, from Paddington and was on shed for servicing. The train reporting numberplate had been removed before the smokebox door was opened and is propped up against the wall near a small seat made from an old sleeper, for use by the disposal men between servicing engines. *R. W. Hinton*

Above:
Six 4-6-0s on the coaling line at Laira shed stand beside 'Grange' class 4-6-0 No 6878 *Longford Grange,* 17 July 1960. Laira Junction signalbox can be seen in the distance below the Embankment Road bridge. On a summer Saturday evening it was usual for the coaling line to stretch out beyond the bridge. *R. C. Riley*

Above:
The Laira shed pilot, '1361' class 0-6-0ST No 1363, awaits its turn on the coaling line alongside 'Hall' class 4-6-0 No 4980 *Wrottesley Hall* on 30 April 1963. This saddle tank is now preserved at the Didcot Railway Centre. *R. C. Riley*

Left:
'9400' class 0-6-0PT No 8426 stands on one of the roads which led from the coaling line to the roundhouse at Laira, on 15 June 1952. Empty coal wagons occupy the end of the ramp line on the coaling stage, and the pump house is to the right of the locomotive. It is sited at the original level as most of Laira shed was constructed on filled ground, access being gained by a steep flight of steps. *Maurice Dart collection*

Below:
A general view of the part of the yard at Laira shed, viewed from outside the roundhouse, with '6100' class 2-6-2T No 6166 beneath the hoist, the ash removal crane and its attendant wagon, 'Modified Hall' class 4-6-0 No 6972 *Beningbrough Hall*, from Bath Road shed, Bristol, 'Castle' and 'Grange' class 4-6-0s and 'County' class 4-6-0 No 1011 *County of Chester*, also from Bath Road shed, seen 27 June 1960. *R. W. Hinton*

Above:
'8750' class 0-6-0PT No 4658 has just propelled a string of loaded coal wagons up the ramp to the coaling stage at Laira, creating the exciting and noisy spectacle of the locomotive using maximum effort for a few seconds, on 19 June 1960. *Maurice Dart/The Transport Treasury*

Above right:
'5101' class 2-6-2T No 5148, the last member of the class in service, stands outside the roundhouse at Laira beside the sand house, buffered up to a 'WD' 2-8-0, with oil drums in the foreground, c1958. *Maurice Dart collection*

Right:
One of Laira's auto-engines, '6400' class 0-6-0PT No 6421, is receiving some attention from fitters inside the roundhouse, on 5 August 1959. Notice the lumps of coal on the cab roof, which have missed the bunker. *Maurice Dart collection*

Above:
Standing outside the New shed at Laira in the winter sun in December 1962 is 'King' class 4-6-0 No 6018 *King Henry VI* from Old Oak Common shed, only a few weeks before it was withdrawn from service. *Mike Daly*

Above:
At the top end of the yard at Laira shed is '6400' class 0-6-0PT No 6408 in front of 'Grange' class 4-6-0 No 6854 *Roundhill Grange*. '8750' class 0-6-0PT No 3686 is at the top of the coaler ramp in this 10 April 1960 view. *R. C. Riley*

Above right:
Standing in the yard at Laira shed between the coaler and the roundhouse on 30 August 1961 are '6959' 'Modified Hall' 4-6-0 No 6997 *Bryn-Ivor Hall* from Bath Road shed, Bristol, and 'WD' 2-8-0 No 90355 from Southall shed. *R. C. Riley*

Right:
The 'New' (Long) shed at Laira was gradually taken over for servicing diesels, three lines of which are visible, while three rows of steam locomotives, which include two 'Halls', are standing outside the stores in this 17 July 1963 view. A 'Grange' is just outside one of the entrances to the roundhouse, right. *R. C. Riley*

Left:
'5101' class 2-6-2T No 5195 of Newton Abbot shed is inside Laira's roundhouse on 19 June 1960, standing on the road leading into the 'Factory', with another Large Prairie tank on one side and a Small Prairie tank on the other. *Maurice Dart/The Transport Treasury*

Below left:
The pair of 0-6-0PTs inside the roundhouse at Laira in January 1962 are '6400' class auto-engine No 6438 and '8750' class No 4658, fitted with a snowplough to combat the blizzard conditions prevailing at that time. *Mike Daly*

Below right:
The yard outside the New shed at Laira is seen c1956, with two '4300' class 2-6-0s, one of which is No 6301, and 'Castle' class 4-6-0 No 5059 *Earl St. Aldwyn* from Newton Abbot shed, behind which is 'Hall' class 4-6-0 No 6938 *Corndean Hall*, also from Newton Abbot shed. *R.W. Hinton.*

Above:
Laira was one of the sheds involved in the short-lived scheme to use oil-burning locomotives, so a fuelling point was established along the outside of the New shed, at which 'Hall' class 4-6-0 No 3955 *Haberfield Hall* (ex-No 6949) is standing, hiding most of 'County' class 4-6-0 No 1011 *County of Chester*, from Bath Road shed, Bristol, on 8 August 1948. *R. S. Carpenter Photos*

Left:
'1361' class 0-6-0ST No 1363, the Laira shed pilot, is attached to coal wagons at the top of the coaler ramp on 2 May 1961. *R. C. Riley*

Left:
The Laira shed pilot locomotive, '1361' class 0-6-0ST No 1363, has shunted loaded coal wagons out from Laira yard and is passing Laira Junction signalbox on the way into the shed yard, 30 August 1951.
R. C. Riley

Above:
The top end of the yard at Laira shed on 17 July 1960, with 'County' class 4-6-0 No 1010 *County of Caernarvon* from Swindon shed prominent and '8750' class 0-6-0PT No 3787 on the coaler ramp. On the coaling line are two 4-6-0s, and a 'Hall' class 4-6-0 stands on the up goods line waiting to run out to Laira Junction signalbox and back on to the coaling line. *R. C. Riley*

Below:
Four 4-6-0s, including 'Grange' class No 6800 *Arlington Grange* from Penzance shed, stand in front of the New shed at Laira, c1960. *R. K. Blencowe collection*

Above:
Outside the New shed at Laira, half of which had by now been adapted for use by diesels, in light steam is 'Castle' class 4-6-0 No 5069 *Isambard Kingdom Brunel* on 22 November 1959. *Maurice Dart/ The Transport Treasury*

Above:
With the impending introduction of diesels, part of the New shed at Laira was separated from the rest by a screen, for their exclusive use, and on which work has commenced. Present inside the shed are 'Grange' class 4-6-0 No 6804 *Brockington Grange* from St Philip's Marsh shed, Bristol, 'Castle' class 4-6-0 No 7024 *Powis Castle* from Old Oak Common shed, and '2884' class 2-8-0 No 3862, on 15 July 1957. *British Railways Western Region*

Left:
Stored inside the New shed at Laira in August 1962 are several locomotives including three '4500' class and one '4575' class 2-6-2Ts, the latter being No 5568 which is on the left. On the right is '1361' class 0-6-0ST No 1363. These had not yet been withdrawn from service. *G. W. Sharpe & Co/ Maurice Dart collection*

Above:
Recently ex works, '4700' class 2-8-0 No 4705 stands near the throat of the yard at Laira shed on 25 September 1960. *R. C. Riley*

Above:
'4575' class 2-6-2T No 5511 stands alongside the breakdown train in the yard at Laira shed. A 'Hall' class 4-6-0 waits to go off shed as a pair of Type 2 diesel-hydraulics come on shed on 30 August 1961. *R. C. Riley*

Left:
The sub-shed at Millbay Docks, Plymouth, with its typical GWR water tank and a breakdown train stabled outside with a shunter's riding truck. Despite the shed having closed in 1955, the adjacent sidings and water tank were still in use in this 25 September 1961 photograph. *R. S. Carpenter Photos*

Plymouth Docks

This one-road shed was inside Millbay Docks and was used until 1955 to stable one of the '1361' class 0-6-0STs overnight on weekdays.

Princetown

The one-road shed here was situated behind the goods shed and yard and was used to stable the branch locomotive, usually a '4400' or later a '4500' class 2-6-2T, overnight and at weekends. It had the distinction of being situated higher above sea level than any other GWR shed.

Left:
With Dartmoor as a backdrop on 31 August 1949, '4500' class 2-6-2T No 4531 stands by the coaling stage at Princetown shed. The shed's coal supply is in wagons behind the loco, which has not yet gained a smokebox numberplate and carries a barely discernible LA shed stencil, just to the left of the front step. This locomotive was withdrawn six months after this photograph was taken. *Maurice Dart collection*

Right:
One of the most remote sheds on the GWR was this structure at the moorland terminus at Princetown, at which the branch locomotive was stabled, seen on 13 April 1936. The water tank is situated above the shed entrance, but the coaling stage was several yards away to the left, served by a siding which also led to a turntable. Although this photograph was taken before World War 2, little changed over the ensuing 20 years. *W. A. Camwell/ Maurice Dart collection*

Launceston

This small shed, containing one road, was very stoutly constructed and could accommodate two tank locomotives, being used to do so overnight and at weekends. During 1959/60 this shed gained some notoriety as a real GWR stronghold. Several of the Small Prairie tanks, which were sub-shedded here from Laira (usually one loco), appeared after a weekend sojourn here carrying GWR-style buffer beam numbers in gold and also having an 'LA' shed stencil on the side of their frames near the front pony truck. Locomotives so treated were Nos 4549/90/91/92.

Right:
The sub-shed at Launceston GW could accommodate two tank locomotives, and here '4575' class 2-6-2T No 5532 is outside, beside the water tank. The line beside the shed is curving around to reach the erstwhile GWR station, with the ex-SR station out of sight to the left, in December 1959.
R. S. Carpenter Photos

Above:
The ex-GWR shed and water tank are visible in the background in this 2 May 1961 view as '4575' class 2-6-2T No 5541 stands on the running line immediately east of the ex-SR station at Launceston. *R. C. Riley*

83E St Blazey SBLZ/ST B/SBZ/83E/84B

This unique, nine-road semi-roundhouse was always an interesting shed to visit as locomotives seemed to be tucked away in various sidings all around it. Also, three of the roads extended through the shed into the 'Factory'.

My first attempt at visiting the shed was a failure. A friend and I had set off from Plymouth on a Sunday morning in 1950 and, having been around the sheds at Penzance and Truro successfully, we detrained at Par and found our way to the shed entrance in heavy rain, which had just commenced. Well, it was an English summer. Standing outside the entrance was the foreman who absolutely declined our request to visit the shed, so a pair of very wet and disappointed enthusiasts returned to the station, and to Plymouth. We were not aware then that an alternative entrance to the shed existed.

I succeeded in going around the shed several times over the next few years, but when I was transferred to St Austell to work early in 1956, and as I was lodging there during the week, I soon made my way out to the shed one evening armed with my camera. I went directly to the office and my heart fell into my boots, for sitting at the desk was the very same foreman who had refused us entry six years previously. I introduced myself and explained that I was now living in the area and was hoping to photograph every tank locomotive in Cornwall, and also any fresh ones that might arrive. Obviously, to do so would require many visits to the various sheds in order to find the different locomotives in photographable positions.

Above left:
Class 4200 2-8-0T No 4273 stands beside '5101' class 2-6-2T No 5193 in the yard, in front of the coaler at St Blazey shed awaiting their next duties, on 20 July 1960. *R. C. Riley*

Above right:
Class 8750 0-6-0PT No 9655 sits in one of the bays inside the unusual nine-road roundhouse at St Blazey where it is undergoing some light repairs to its smokebox, revealing the boiler tubeplate holes, on 20 July 1960. *R. C. Riley*

Above:
St Blazey shed, seen from across the river on 23 April 1960, showing the nine-road roundhouse-type building, the hoist and part of the wagon works. Locomotives visible are '5101' class 2-6-2T No 4167, '7400' class 0-6-0PT No 7446, '5205' class 2-8-0T No 5264 and North British Type 2 diesel-hydraulic No D6308 which is on the vacuum-operated turntable. An old tender, probably used for sludge, is on the left. *B. W. L. Brooksbank/ Initial Photographics*

Left:
The coaling line at St Blazey shed holds '4300' class 2-6-0 No 7316 from Exeter shed, and '1400' class 0-4-2T No 1419, which was the Fowey branch auto-engine, on 7 August 1956. *Maurice Dart/The Transport Treasury*

Right:
Having its tender coal supply replenished at St Blazey shed is '4300' class 2-6-0 No 6397, with wagons above it on the coaling stage ramp, on 10 July 1955.
R. S. Carpenter Photos

He asked me several questions and then told me that he was Mr Dunn, the shedmaster, and was quite happy for me to visit whenever I wished. I was amazed but very pleased, and thanked him for the offer. Over the years I met successive shedmasters, such as George Thomas (an ex-Laira foreman) and Fred Bishop, all of whom were equally co-operative. Latterly, there was a driver who acted as relief foreman called 'Bolshie' Granger. His nickname reflected his general attitude to everything, but even he let me around a few times after grumbling that 'You people are a pain in the neck'.

St Blazey could spring a surprise sometimes, such as when I visited one Saturday afternoon (5 September 1959) and found Nos 1627 (85B), 7761 (83C), 8409 (83G), 8713 (84E) and 8737 (84E) on shed. To find five visiting pannier tanks was unheard of, but several of the shed's own locomotives were away at works or under repair in the shed. Actually, four of these were officially transferred to the shed for periods of between four months and two years, but No 7761 returned soon after to Exeter. The shed maintained a 100 per cent GWR allocation until diesels arrived. After closure to steam, three Small Prairie tanks (Nos 4564, 5518 and 5531) remained stored behind the coaling stage for about 12 months. I visited the shed 12 times.

Sunday, 23 August 1953		**Shed Codes**
Class 1000 4-6-0	1021 (83D)	83D Laira
Class 1400 0-4-2T	1419	83G Penzance
Class 1600 0-6-0PT	1626	
Class 2021 0-6-0PT	2097	
Class 2181 0-6-0PT	2182	
Class 4200 2-8-0T	4247	
Class 4500 2-6-2T	4523/52/68	
Class 4575 2-6-2T	4585, 5519/21	
Class 4900 4-6-0	5926	
Class 5101 2-6-2T	5193	
Class 5700 0-6-0PT	7709/15, 8719 (83D), 8733	
Class 6400 0-6-0PT	6407 (83D)	
Class 6800 4-6-0	6826 (83G)	
Class 7400 0-6-0PT	7446	
Class 7800 4-6-0	7816	
Class 8750 0-6-0PT	3635, 3705, 9671 (83D), 9673, 9755	

Left:
On the vacuum-operated turntable at St Blazey, '5700' class 0-6-0PT No 8702 is about to be positioned to enter the shed on 23 April 1956. The disposal man is connecting the vacuum pipe to the locomotive to operate the turntable. *Maurice Dart*

Below left:
Lined up alongside St Blazey shed are '1600' class 0-6-0PT No 1664 and '4500' class 2-6-2Ts Nos 4552 and 4559, seen on 23 April 1956. The tall building in the background, above the engineering shops, was once the board room of the Cornwall Minerals Railway. *Maurice Dart/ The Transport Treasury*

Below right:
The china clay branch lines abounded in sharp curves which caused considerable wear to locomotive driving wheels, therefore providing constant work for the hoist at St Blazey shed as these were attended to. This is evidenced here with three 0-6-0PTs, two of which — '5700' class No 8702 and '7400' class No 7446 — have wheels removed, while '8750' class No 3790 awaits similar attention on an adjacent road with another locomotive, on 5 June 1961. *Maurice Dart/The Transport Treasury*

Monday, 5 June 1961

Class 1600 0-6-0PT	1624/26/64
Class 4200 2-8-0T	4273
Class 4500 2-6-2T	4564
Class 4575 2-6-2T	5539, 5545 (83G – on loan), 5553/70
Class 5700 0-6-0PT	7715, 8702/19/33/37
Class 6400 0-6-0PT	6413 (83D)
Class 6800 4-6-0	6814 (83G), 6825/75
Class 7400 0-6-0PT	7446
Class 8750 0-6-0PT	3790, 4665, 9655, 9716/55
Class 1400 0-4-2T	1468
Type 2 diesel B-B	D6307/15 (both 83D)
Type 4 diesel B-B	D831 (83D)
Diesel 0-6-0	D4005/08

Shed Codes

83C Exeter; 83D Laira, Plymouth; 83G Penzance; 84E Tyseley; 85B Gloucester (and Lydney sub-shed)

Above right:
A portion of the roundhouse at St Blazey seen on 26 May 1957, with two 0-6-0PTs, '5700' class No 8702 inside and '7400' class No 7446, together with '5101' class 2-6-2T No 5193, which was allocated to Laira but seemed to spend a great deal of time at St Blazey as it was a regular on a pick-up goods from Tavistock Junction yard.
R. S. Carpenter Photos

Rright:
A view looking south from the front of the shed at St Blazey, on 15 July 1958, showing part of the yard with the ash crane in front of the coaling stage, which is topped with a water tank. A pair of 0-6-0PTs, '5700' class No 8733 and '8750' class No 3635, are by the turntable.
The Transport Treasury

Left:
Two locomotives, '4300' class 2-6-0 No 6301 from Laira shed and '4575' class 2-6-2T No 5523, which was awaiting withdrawal, stand in the shed yard at St Blazey on 22 May 1960 with the wagon works building in the background. Numerous wheelsets from wagons were — and still are — a feature of St Blazey shed yard. *Maurice Dart/The Transport Treasury*

Below left:
Inside the roundhouse at St Blazey are two '4500' class 2-6-2Ts, Nos 4569 and 4505, seen on 1 June 1955. *R. K. Blencowe collection*

Below:
With the arrival of diesels imminent, modifications were carried out to St Blazey shed to provide suitable facilities for servicing them. This was taking place while '4500' class 2-6-2T No 4565 was inside the roundhouse receiving some attention, for which it has been raised up on jacks, on 31 July 1958. *British Railways Western Region*

Above:
An area not normally photographed at St Blazey shed, showing the block which housed the various engineering departments, the sidings which held wagons containing the shed's coal supply, and the inclined ramp to the coaling stage, on 10 December 1958. *British Railways Western Region.*

Above:
On 18 July 1960 Class 4500 2-6-2T No 4552 waits with a short goods at Moorswater, alongside the two-road locomotive shed on the remnant of the line which once led northwards to Cheesewring and Caradon. *R. C. Riley*

Above:
The view from a train crossing the viaduct at Moorswater on 9 July 1960, showing (left to right) the erstwhile carriage and wagon works, the water tank and the locomotive shed. Some china clay wagons stand on a siding to the left of the buildings, and, to the right of centre, a pair of lime kilns are visible. *R. C. Riley*

Moorswater

This two-road shed was visible from a main-line train as it crossed Moorswater Viaduct, just west of Liskeard, and could be reached by walking along a footpath from Coombe Junction Halt. There was just the requisite time for this while the branch train proceeded to Looe and returned. Overnight and at weekends, one or two small Prairie tanks would be sub-shedded here from St Blazey. I made two visits to the shed which was made famous by the presence of the firebox wrapper plate from Liskeard & Caradon Railway 0-6-0ST *Caradon* which was fitted with a seat and a door and placed over a stream beside the shed to act as a toilet. It survives in preservation on the end of the platform at Bodmin General station.

Above:
The two-road sub-shed at Moorswater, with '4500' class 2-6-2T No 4569 inside in June 1954. The water tank is on the left and in the left background is the defunct carriage shed. The roofless coaling stage is in front of the water tank and on the right is *Caradon's* firebox. *Rail Archive Stephenson*

Sunday, 5 July 1959

Class 4500 2-6-2T	4552

Wednesday, 7 June 1961

Class 4575 2-6-2T	5518

Bodmin

This was a one-road shed at the end of the platform at Bodmin General, and normally stabled a pair of Small Prairie tanks, sub-shedded from St Blazey, overnight and at weekends. I saw the shed around 10 times, there being no need to go into it.

Tuesday, 26 June 1956

Class 4500 2-6-2T	4508

Saturday, 11 June 1960

Class 4500 2-6-2T	4552

Below left:
Small Prairie '4500' class 2-6-2T No 4526 rests beside the coaling stage at the small sub-shed at Bodmin, GWR, with the typical water tank well to the fore, on 22 June 1956. *Maurice Dart/The Transport Treasury*

Below right:
'4500' class 2-6-2T No 4559 is running round its train at Bodmin General with the one-road locomotive shed, water tank and coaling stage on the right, on 16 July 1958. *The Transport Treasury*

Above:
The shed yard and coaler at Truro, seen from the road which passes the station, with the end of the turntable just visible on the left. Locomotives present include 'Manor' and 'Hall' class 4-6-0s, a '9400' class 0-6-0PT and a '4575' class 2-6-2T, which are standing around the breakdown train. The extension to the shed building, to facilitate servicing diesel multiple-units, is apparent, with the front of one protruding in this 22 July 1960 view. *R. C. Riley*

Right:
Class 4575 2-6-2T No 5515 stands over one of the ash pits in the shed yard at Truro, being serviced for its next duty. An ex-LNER parcels coach is in the stock sidings, 8 April 1960. *R. C. Riley*

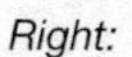

Right:
'4500' class 2-6-2T No 4566 from Penzance shed on 23 July 1960. The last locomotive to be overhauled at Newton Abbot Works, it stands at the front of Truro shed yard. 350hp diesel shunter No D3509 is the goods yard pilot. *R. C. Riley*

Left:
A general view of Truro shed with 'Hall' class 4-6-0 No 6911 *Holker Hall* from St Blazey shed, '4300' class 2-6-0 No 5376 and a 2-6-2T in the yard sidings 'County' class 4-6-0 No 1023 *County of Oxford* and a 2-6-2T are outside the shed, along with '8750' class 0-6-0PT No 3702. Standing outside the one-road 'Factory', '4575' class 2-6-2T No 5562 has its smokebox door open on 22 March 1959.
R. K. Blencowe collection

 Truro — TR/83F/84C from 9/9/63

This shed was at the end of the yard, southwest of the station. An excellent view of the shed yard was gained from the long footbridge which crossed all lines, but to reach the shed required a circular walk either from the end of the footbridge or by going up the hill from the station and passing over Higher Town Tunnel. The complex consisted of a three-road locomotive shed with offices and stores, a one-road 'Factory', and a three-road wagon shop. During 1959, in preparation for the soon-to-arrive diesel locomotives, the three roads were reduced to two and the shed was extended in length, but the depot closed completely in October 1965.

It maintained a 100 per cent GWR allocation until the arrival of diesels and closed to steam in March 1962, but almost immediately a surprise arrived in the form of withdrawn 0-6-0PT No 8408 to act as a stationary boiler. This remained until at least April 1963, but had departed by February 1964. As this locomotive had been shedded at 87C and 87D when in service, it was quite a turn-up for the books.

Other unusual locomotives appeared when the turntable at Penzance shed was out of action during August 1946, December 1948 and spring 1955. Large Prairie tanks from a variety of sheds were then drafted in to work in place of tender locomotives. Local enthusiasts had field days on these occasions.

The coaling arrangements were rather unusual for a GWR shed as a grab bucket ran on a girder from the coaling stage to deposit coal into the locomotive tender or bunker. The foremen here were always friendly, and I visited the shed 10 times.

Sunday, 23 August 1953

Class 1000 4-6-0	1023
Class 4300 2-6-0	6305
Class 4500 2-6-2T	4554
Class 4575 2-6-2T	4588, 5500/15/26/37/62
Class 4900 4-6-0	4985, 5985
Class 5101 2-6-2T	5175 (83D)
Class 6800 4-6-0	6825 (83G), 6873 (83D)
Class 7400 0-6-0PT	7422
Class 9400 0-6-0PT	8404/21/85/86, 9434

Saturday, 6 February 1960

Class 6800 4-6-0	6805, 6826/70 (both 83G)
Class 7800 4-6-0	7806 (83E), 7813
Class 4575 2-6-2T	4587, 5509/38/59/62
Class 5101 2-6-2T	4108
Class 8750 0-6-0PT	3702, 4622
Diesel 0-6-0	D3509 (in Factory)

Shed Codes

83D Laira, Plymouth; 83E St Blazey; 83G Penzance; 87C Danygraig, Swansea; 87D Swansea East Dock

Upper left:
When work was required to be carried out on the turntable at Penzance shed, Large Prairie tanks were drafted in temporarily to Truro from a variety of other sheds, thus making life extremely interesting for local enthusiasts. On one such occasion, 24 May 1956, '5101' class 2-6-2T No 4107 from Landore shed, Swansea, is in the yard in company with 'County' class 4-6-0s Nos 1007 *County of Brecknock* and 1018 *County of Leicester*, from Penzance shed. *Maurice Dart/The Transport Treasury*

Lower left:
The turntable, coaling stage and yard at Truro shed, viewed from a train heading to Penzance, c1959. Two '4575' class 2-6-2Ts are present; No 4587 is being coaled and No 5500 is in the holding sidings, with 'Grange' class 4-6-0 No 6875 *Hindford Grange*, from Penzance shed, next to the breakdown train. The canopy extension to the front of the shed, to facilitate servicing diesel multiple-units, is visible. *N. L. Browne/Maurice Dart collection*

Left:
'4500' class 2-6-2T No 4574 stands at the throat of the shed yard at Truro on 24 July 1950. *R. C. Riley*

Below left:
'Hall' class 4-6-0 No 5915 *Trentham Hall* from Penzance shed is partly on the turntable at Truro shed with a '9400' class 0-6-0PT behind, in this photograph taken on 17 August 1954. The end of the coaling stage ramp is on the right. The locomotive has a shedplate, but carries no smokebox or buffer beam number. *Maurice Dart collection*

Below right:
Work is in progress during construction of the extension to Truro shed, ready to accommodate the soon-to-arrive DMUs. Inside the shed are '4300' class 2-6-0 No 5376 and a '4575' class 2-6-2T on 5 August 1959. *British Railways Western Region*

Falmouth

There was a water tower alongside the site of the shed, where there was now only one road instead of the previous two, and this was used for watering locomotives working the branch.

Right:
Despite the shed at Falmouth having closed in 1925, a pit and watering facilities were retained well into BR days. Only one road served these instead of the two which formerly existed, and the coaling facility had been removed in this August 1948 view. *Joe Moss collection/R. S. Carpenter Photos*

Below:
Four railwaymen are engaged in turning 'Modified Hall' class 4-6-0 No 7916 *Mobberley Hall,* from Laira shed, on the 65ft turntable at Long Rock shed, Penzance, in readiness for working an eastbound train to Plymouth on 29 April 1961. *R. C. Riley*

Left:
Lined up beside the shed at Long Rock, Penzance, are three 'Grange' class 4-6-0s, Nos 6824 *Ashley Grange*, 6825 *Llanvair Grange* and 6826 *Nannerth Grange* on 21 April 1962. *R. K. Blencowe collection*

Right:
Standing over the pits outside Long Rock shed are 'Grange' class 4-6-0s Nos 6801 *Aylburton Grange* and 6800 *Arlington Grange*, seen in June 1952. *R. K. Blencowe collection*

83G Penzance — PZ/83G/84D from 9/63

This consisted of a four-road long shed and a single-road lifting shop and was over a mile from Penzance station. I once tried alighting from a train at Marazion to reach it, but found the walk equally long. It was referred to by the GWR as Ponsondane shed, but locally it was always called Long Rock, and the parcels depot immediately west of the shed was at Ponsondane. On my first visit I skirted the outside of the shed and found the holes in the black wooden fence gave excellent views of locomotives in the shed yard and by the coaling stage. Afterwards, I went through a gap in the fence and entered the rear of the shed, which I walked through. On subsequent visits I always saw the foreman on arrival and was never refused admission.

The shed was 100 per cent GWR allocation in the BR period, but also serviced 'Britannia' Pacifics from Laira, which had worked down. As an aside, it is worth mentioning that in 1944, brand-new Swindon-built LMS-design '8F' class 2-8-0 No 8435 was allocated here for working broccoli trains.

Apart from different members of the same classes, no changes occurred here except for the arrival of new types, such as the '9400' class pannier tanks. As already mentioned under Truro, when the turntable was out of action, a contingent of Large Prairie tanks from all over the system was drafted in for several weeks, these being from '3100', '5101', '6100' and '8100' classes. They came from sheds such as Newton Abbot, Laira, Taunton, Stafford Road, Leamington, Stourbridge, Birkenhead, Worcester, Gloucester, Cheltenham, Ebbw Junction, Neath, Landore and Carmarthen, and were divided between Penzance and Truro sheds. With the arrival of diesels, a screen was erected along the centre of the shed to segregate them from the steam locomotives.
I visited the shed eight times.

Sunday, 23 August 1953

Class 3150 2-6-2T	3187 (83D)
Class 4073 4-6-0	4087, 5023
Class 4500 2-6-2T	4500/48, 4570 (83F), 4574
Class 4900 4-6-0	4958 (82B), 5969, 6913 (83D)
Class 5101 2-6-2T	5196 (83A)
Class 6800 4-6-0	6800/08/09/17/24/36
Class 8750 0-6-0PT	9717
Class 9400 0-6-0PT	8473, 9463

Saturday, 6 February 1960

Class 1000 4-6-0	1006/18
Class 4073 4-6-0	5032 (83A)
Class 4500 2-6-2T	4566
Class 4575 2-6-2T	5541
Class 4900 4-6-0	4908, 4967 (83D), 6933, 6940 (83A), 6945
Class 6800 4-6-0	6800/08/16, 6823 (83F), 6826/45/75
Class 8750 0-6-0PT	9748
Class 9400 0-6-0PT	8473
Type 2 diesel B-B	D6309/13 (both 83D)

Shed Codes
82B St Philip's Marsh, Bristol; 83A Newton Abbot; 83D Laira, Plymouth; 83F Truro

Above:
Long Rock shed, after a screen had been erected down the centre to segregate the soon-to-arrive diesel locomotives from their steam compatriots. Four 4-6-0s, two of which are 'Granges', are outside the front of the shed in this 16 September 1959 photograph.
British Railways Western Region

Left:
Long Rock motive power depot, Penzance, on 17 March 1959, showing the running shed, 'Factory', boiler house and pump house. The locomotives present in the yard are 'Hall' class 4-6-0 No 4931 *Hanbury Hall*, 'Manor' 4-6-0 No 7820 *Dinmore Manor* from Laira shed, '4575' 2-6-2T No 5524, '4500' 2-6-2T No 4563, and '9400' 0-6-0PT No 9463.
British Railways Western Region

6826

Helston

The small, one-road shed here was just off the end of the platform and stabled one Small Prairie tank overnight and at weekends.

St Ives

This single-road shed was separated from the station by the curving, 106yd-long St Ives Viaduct. One Small Prairie tank was stabled overnight and at weekends.

Left:
A pair of 'Grange' class 4-6-0s, the front one being No 6826 *Nannerth Grange*, are seen in the yard at Long Rock shed, Penzance, on 22 April 1961. *R. C. Riley*

Upper right:
The sub-shed at Helston, with a pair of '4500' class 2-6-2Ts in view in the summer of 1958. No 4554 is outside the shed in front of a wagon loaded with coal, while No 4540 is shunting on the opposite side of the running line. *Norman Simmons/Hugh Davies Photographs*

Lower right:
St Ives station with the goods shed behind it and the one-road locomotive shed situated remotely on a short spur at the far end of the viaduct, left, with the water tank up on the bank in front of the shed. Although taken at an earlier period, this scene remained largely unchanged into the 1950s, apart from the clerestory stock. *Maurice Dart collection*

The Engine Sheds
INDUSTRIAL

Left:
The locomotive shed of the 4ft 6in gauge Lee Moor Tramway at Torycombe, near Lee Moor village, still contained the pair of Peckett 0-4-0STs in May 1955, 10 years after the upper section of the line had closed. *Maurice Dart/ The Transport Treasury*

Above:
The Admiralty dockyard at Devonport possessed two locomotive sheds. Inside the South Yard shed, which had a roof high enough to accommodate a steam crane, is 0-4-0ST No 11 (Barclay 1380, built 1914), seen in the early 1950s. *Mike Daly*

Above right:
The North Yard locomotive shed at Devonport Dockyard with No 12 (Avonside 1690, built 1915), outside and to the left, No 13 (Barclay 1397, built 1915) and either No 17 or No 18, both of which were Barclays, in the early 1950s. *Mike Daly*

Lee Moor

Within two hours of starting work for English Clays' Lovering & Pochin at Lee Moor, I was taken into the locomotive shed of the 4ft 6in gauge Lee Moor Tramway at Torycombe to see the pair of locomotives which had worked the section of the line between the two inclines. On my second day at work there, I took my camera and flashgun with me to record the scene. The locomotives had been locked inside since 1948. I made several subsequent visits with groups of enthusiasts. Both are preserved: No 1 at the Wheal Martyn China Clay Museum near St Austell, and No 2 at the South Devon Railway,

Monday, 18 May 1953

Lee Moor No 1	Peckett 783 (1899) 0-4-0ST
Lee Moor No 2	Peckett 784 (1899) 0-4-0ST

HM Dockyard, Devonport

This extensive system possessed two locomotive sheds. The main one in the North Yard was a three-road building, while that in the South Yard had two roads, but it had a lofty roof as it was also intended to house a self-propelled steam crane. As I was not employed by this establishment I regret that I was never able to visit these sheds.

March Mills

A locomotive was kept at English Clays' Lovering & Pochins works at Marsh Mills but the only facility provided was an inspection pit which in later years gained a type of makeshift canopy.

Par Harbour

This standard-gauge, one-road shed came under the jurisdiction of English China Clays and stabled and maintained the locomotives which worked around the harbour and associated lines. I visited the shed several times with parties of enthusiasts.

Wednesday, 10 July 1957

	Bagnall 2572 (1937) 0-4-0ST
Alfred	Bagnall 3058 (1953) 0-4-0ST
	Sentinel 6520 (1927) 4wVBT (out of use behind shed)

Above:
The shed at Falmouth Docks is seen on 17 April 1963, containing a pair of 0-4-0STs which are No 3 Hawthorn Leslie No 3648, built 1926, and No 6 Peckett No 1530, built 1919. *Maurice Dart*

Falmouth Docks

I managed to obtain permission to visit here once and was taken round under close supervision and security, as visits were rarely permitted. The system possessed a one-road shed which would hold two locomotives, any repair work being carried out in a separate workshop which dealt with all the equipment on site.

Wednesday, 17 April 1963

FD&HB No 3	Hawthorn, Leslie 3597 (1926) 0-4-0ST (in the shed)
FD&HB No 5	Hudswell, Clarke 1632 (1929) 0-4-0ST (in the works)
FD&HB No 6	Peckett 1530 (1919) 0-4-0ST (in the shed)

The other locomotive (No 4, Hawthorn, Leslie 3670 of 1927) was out working.

Left:
The Port of Par operated a pair of 0-4-0STs on its internal system, both of which had cut-down mountings and cabs to permit them to pass beneath a bridge under the main line of the GWR, west of Par station. *Alfred* (Bagnall 3058, built 1953) stands outside the locomotive shed at Par Harbour on 15 June 1977. *Tom Heavyside*

Penlee Quarry, Newlyn

I visited here, again accompanied by Mike Daly. We travelled by train from St Budeaux to Penzance and walked to the quarry where we found the locomotive shed with a small diesel outside, together with a preserved steam locomotive. We wandered around the exterior of the two-road shed which served the 2ft gauge system and I discovered a small opening at one side of the rear door. Being quite thin I was just able to squeeze myself through this to identify the locomotives therein. This was my only visit to this location.

Sunday, 18 November 1956

Penlee	Freudenstein 73 (1901) 0-4-0WT (preserved)
Penlee LM3	Hunslet 2666 (1942) 4wD
Penlee LM1	Kerr, Stuart 4468 (1930) 4wDM
J. W. Jenkin LM40	Ruston & Hornsby 375315 (1954) 4wDM
T. W. Lewis LM39	Ruston & Hornsby 375316 (1954) 4wDM

Also, a further three four-wheel diesels, which carried no identification.

Exeter Gasworks

To shunt the internal system of sidings, two locomotives were kept here in a one-road shed near the entrance to the complex, which I visited once with my friend Mike Daly. We went by train from Plymouth, changed at Newton Abbot and proceeded via the Teign Valley line to St Davids from where we walked to the site, Mike knowing where to find the shed.

Saturday, 15 March 1958
Peckett 2031 (1942) 0-4-0ST
Peckett 2074 (1946) 0-4-0ST

Upper right:
Standing outside Penlee Quarry locomotive shed, attached to a tipper wagon, is 4wDM *J. W. Jenkin* LM40 Ruston & Hornsby No 375315, built in 1954. The photograph was taken on 29 June 1961. *Maurice Dart collection*

Lower left:
By the foreshore west of Newlyn village, near the locomotive shed of the Penlee Quarry Railway, on 18 November 1956, was this 0-4-0WT Freudenstein 73, *Penlee*, built in 1901. The psuedo-television aerial on the dome was an adornment fitted when the locomotive participated in a local carnival procession. *Maurice Dart*